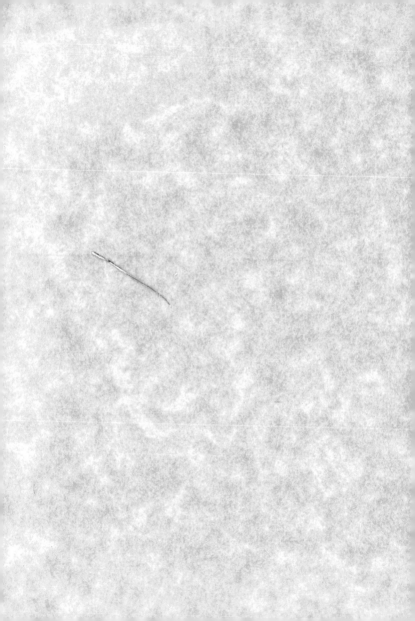

The TEN COMMANDMENTS of Self-Esteem

✳

The TEN COMMANDMENTS of Self-Esteem

Catherine Cardinal, Ph.D.

Andrews McMeel Publishing

Kansas City

www.andrewsmcmeel.com

98 99 00 01 02 QUF 10 9 8 7 6 5 4 3 2 1

Designed by Kathryn Parise

LIBRARY OF CONGRESS CATALOGING-IN-PUBLICATION DATA
Cardinal, Catherine, 1953–
The ten commandments of self-esteem / Catherine Cardinal.
p. cm.
ISBN 0-8362-5196-2 (hardcover)
1. Self-esteem.
BF697.5.S46C36 1998
158. 1—dc21 97-41455
CIP

✻ ✻

This book is dedicated to my clients,
who over the years have been my greatest teachers.

✻ ✻

Contents

Acknowledgments

To Daniel Bushnell . . . Thank you for your magnificent editing, your literary flair, and for adding the whipped-cream and cherry to this book. You are my dear, dear friend.

To Kim Cardinal, Dr. Mary Elizabeth Ensign, Sarab Atma Kaur, Dr. Sara Gordon, Patrice Karst, and Dr. Bobbi Liberton for being my soul sisters. Thanks for your years of support and unconditional love.

To my agent, Frank Weimann, for "getting" what this book is about, seeing its value, and believing in it and me. Thanks to you my first publishing experience was a joy.

To my editor, Jake Morrissey, for your suggestions, which added richness to the Commandments.

To Rachel Carr and Patrice Messina for your patience and fabulous typing skills.

※ ※

To Robert Proden for giving me the push to get this written, and Gary Peattie at DeVorss for his belief in the book.

To Dr. Morris Netherton and Dr. Alice Givens for fostering my interest in psychology and changing my life's course.

To Dr. Pat Clawson, Kathleen Madigan, Rev. Michael Beckwith, Laurence Fremy, Scott Catamas, Gary Frederick, and Bill Glasser for their caring, interest, time, and effort.

And to Roger . . . for always believing in me.

※ ※

THE TEN COMMANDMENTS OF SELF-ESTEEM

I.

THOU SHALT NOT CONSORT WITH PEOPLE WHO MAKE THEE FEEL BAD ABOUT THYSELF.

II.

THOU SHALT CEASE TRYING TO MAKE SENSE OUT OF CRAZY BEHAVIOR.

III

THOU SHALT NOT KEEP COMPANY WITH THOSE MORE DYSFUNCTIONAL THAN THYSELF.

IV.

TRUST THY BODY ALL THE DAYS OF THY LIFE (THY MIND DOTH FORNICATE WITH THEE).

V.
THOU HAST PERMISSION AT ALL TIMES
TO SAY "NO," TO CHANGE THY MIND, AND TO EXPRESS
THY TRUE FEELINGS.

VI.
WHAT IS NOT RIGHT FOR THEE IS NOT RIGHT
FOR THY BRETHREN.

VII.
THOU SHALT NOT GIVE BEYOND THINE
OWN CAPACITY.

VIII.
WHAT THY BRETHREN THINK OF THEE
MATTERETH NAUGHT.

IX.
WHEREVER THOU ART, THEREIN ALSO IS THE PARTY.

X.
THOU SHALT SING THINE OWN PRAISES
ALL THE DAYS OF THY LIFE.

Introduction

I n the ancient days, the Lord looked down upon his children and saw a humanity suffering from selfishness, greed, and ignorance of universal laws. He saw fit to call upon Moses to receive his Ten Commandments and share them with his people. For thousands of years these have served as a guide for men and women in their behavior and ways of treating one another.

Today, if the Lord were to cast the same gaze upon his children, he would see humanity suffering still from numerous faults. Toward the top of that list is a sense of low self-esteem. Those who suffer from this flaw would be making poor choices in business and relationships, and they would be undermining their real contributions to life.

This problem of self-esteem is epidemic and has many roots. Chiefly, it seems to be most contagious between parent and child. Whatever beliefs, habits, and ideas we were given as children, we tend to pass on to our children—unless, of course, we are fortunate enough to become aware of these issues in time and choose to do something about them. There are few manuals on how to parent and how to achieve high self-esteem—the course is being written today by the thousands of us who are learning to deal with our own issues.

I have not seen a burning bush recently—nor have I heard from Moses in a few years. But from years of practicing psychotherapy, having hundreds of people confront their issues and bare their souls on my couch, I have worked intensely with this issue of low self-esteem.

I've seen how prevalent, how hidden, and how devastating it can be. And along the way, I've also discovered some practical techniques and suggestions that have helped countless clients.

I want to share some of these with you.

I have structured this book with one major topic in each section. As the original Ten Commandments were aimed at correcting or preventing sins, I have included techniques and examples to help the reader improve behaviors that damage the various aspects of self-esteem. One of the original meanings of the word "sin" was an archery term meaning "to miss the mark." Penances were imposed to bring people's behavior back in line, back on target. Here I've given "Resolutions," helpful hints to bring our thinking and emotions back to where they should be: to make us highly effective, dynamic people who have a strong sense of self-esteem.

Let us begin the journey to healthier self-esteem.

COMMANDMENT I

Thou shalt not consort with people who make thee feel bad about thyself.

Are there people you know who make you feel great whenever you're around them, who make you feel cared for, listened to, and valued for just being who you are? Are there others who make you feel guilty and inadequate, who make you doubt yourself, who truly would like you to be someone else? These people can leave you feeling drained, exhausted, and insecure.

Healthy self-esteem is paying attention to how others make us feel—and then choosing those with whom we spend time. It may require courage to move away from negative people, especially if they've been in our lives for some time. But letting go of others can be very empowering for ourselves. And the price of not doing it is to shut down emotionally, to have less energy, and to deny our true feelings.

Choosing our companions wisely forces us to listen to our deepest feelings while watching carefully how others treat us. Sometimes, people appear to be our friends on the surface, and say and do all the "right things," yet their real intent may not be in our best interest. Other times a true friend may care deeply enough to tell us some truth that may hurt. How others make us feel is the barometer we use to develop discernment. Just always know that you deserve to be surrounded by positive people, loving friends, and situations that enhance your life every day.

A client of mine dated a man who seemed to possess all the qualities she was searching for. She would call me, great excitement in her voice, certain that she had found "the one"—until the day she first went to his apartment.

In his bedroom he had pictures of numerous women displayed on a bulletin board, many in bikinis, some of whom he proudly identified as previous lovers. My client felt very uncomfortable about this and asked him to remove the pictures. Their communication was open enough that she felt safe to tell him how insecure those pictures made her feel.

He responded by telling her that she had a self-esteem problem and she would need to "get over" the pictures. His argument was that these women were all friends of his and should pose no threat to her. She was confused by this, and began to question her own self-esteem, as he had suggested.

In talking with friends and in therapy sessions, she came to understand that she had a right to feel exactly as she did and he was out of line to disregard her feelings. As she began to express her feelings more clearly to him, his comments no longer made her feel bad about herself.

She eventually chose to end the relationship. And she later found out that this man was having affairs with other women during the time they were together.

Why do negative people exist in our lives? Because we invite them in psychologically. Since our lives are largely a printout of our inner-core beliefs, if we didn't have doubts about our own worth, we simply would not listen to others' negativity. Learn to recognize those people who consistently make you feel bad or uncomfortable.

Resolutions:

1. Make a list of every significant person in your life. Next to each name, describe how he or she makes you feel about yourself on a consistent basis.
2. For each of those who makes you feel bad, ask yourself, "Does this person continue to serve a constructive purpose in my life?"
3. If any person does not, then make the conscious choice to either transform that relationship or end it. If you cannot physically leave the relationship, you can at least emotionally distance yourself.

COMMANDMENT II

Thou shalt cease trying to make sense out of crazy behavior.

Have you ever found yourself trying to understand another person's behavior that just didn't make sense to you? You may even have been shocked by it. But try as you may to figure out why he did what he did, it just doesn't make sense to you. Your brain goes "tilt" and still you have no answers. It feels "crazy" to you.

We all behave the way we do for our own reasons. We are the result of all of our history plus our decisions. This creates a matrix of patterns and beliefs that governs our behavior. People who are inconsistent in their actions have inconsistencies in their past. And to uncover and heal the roots of these patterns usually requires a professional—a therapist—and may take time. If you assume the task of figuring it all out yourself and healing them, you are probably going to waste too much time—yours.

When we are drawn to chaos it is usually because of the authority figures we experienced as children. Some examples of "crazy makers" are alcoholics, religious fanatics, rageaholics, and perfectionists. As children we observed their inconsistent behavior, blamed it on ourselves, and tried to fix ourselves so their patterns would change. But since that didn't happen, we got confused, felt inadequate, and planted the seeds of unhealthy self-esteem.

The lesson is: Stop trying to figure it out! You will only become confused and frustrated.

A client of mine, Liz, was visiting her mother for Christmas when her cousin Bob showed up to spend the holiday with them. Liz had not seen her cousin for more than sixteen years. Her mother encouraged the two of them to spend time together. "Why don't you two go out and get reacquainted? I have plenty to do here at home."

For the next few days, Bob and Liz spent a lot of time together.

One afternoon, Bob's sister Mary was due to arrive to join the three of them. When it came time to pick her up at the airport, the mother's attitude suddenly shifted, and she began to attack Liz. "Well, it would have been nice if you had spent some time with me, but you spent it all with Bob. So now I'm going to pick up Mary and we're going out on the town. You and Bob can stay home for a change." With that she stormed out of the house, slamming the front door behind her.

Liz felt very guilty, hurt, and confused by all this. Bob then explained to her: "You shouldn't feel bad at all. You did exactly what your mother asked you to do, and you did nothing wrong. She's nuts."

Ask others to explain their behavior to you, and their reasons for doing it. You have the right to do this. By asking, you are stopping the futile process of trying to figure them out. You remove yourself from a no-win situation.

Perhaps they cannot explain or change their behavior (for example, an alcoholic who keeps on drinking, or a liar who continues to make excuses), but you no longer will doubt yourself. You will know it is their problem, not yours. Healthy self-esteem seeks a consistent and sane environment where shock, confusion, and chaos are at a minimum.

Resolutions:

1. Observe how often you are presented with confusing behavior (actions that just don't make sense to you).
2. Bring this to the attention of the other person (say, for example, "You know, you really confused me when you . . . "). Ask him or her to explain it to you. Listen carefully to how the person justifies the behavior and/or assumes responsibility for the confusion. Check the person's commitment to change.
3. See if his or her behavior changes in a reasonable period of time. If not, then reexamine the value of that relationship in your life, and if necessary, move on.

COMMANDMENT III

Thou shalt not keep company with those more dysfunctional than thyself.

※ ※

Do you remember having a best buddy as a kid? Someone you could go on adventures with, get into trouble with, share your deepest thoughts and feelings with? You would play together, laugh together—perhaps the same sentences would even come out of your mouths together. The reason you got along so well is that you shared the same values. You understood each other.

As we grow into adults, our needs and values become more complex and it becomes more difficult to find such a "best buddy." So we often settle for friends and companions who are not a healthy match for us—and as a result our self-esteem begins to erode.

One of my neighbors, Keith, told me a story about his

※ ※

mailman. It seems there was a woman on the next street who was confiding to several neighbors that she and the mailman were building a relationship. She exuberantly told them about the wonderful conversations they were sharing and how close they were becoming.

Keith, who happened to be a good friend of the mailman, kidded him one day about his new relationship. The mailman responded with absolute shock, saying: "What relationship? Every day when I deliver the mail to her, she meets me on the front porch and gives me a glass of iced tea. I chat with her long enough to finish the tea, which I look forward to, and then I proceed on my route. That's all there is to it!"

It was immediately obvious that this woman was creating a romantic fantasy out of a light conversation. The mailman stopped accepting the iced tea, and the woman retreated into her house at mail delivery time. She later revealed to her neighbors that the mailman had "dumped her," adding, "Aren't men terrible?"

For the mailman, it had been a refreshing break from a tedious route; for the woman, it was a burgeoning love affair. Although the mailman would have been open to being her friend, he knew that cutting off all communication with this person was the healthiest option.

As we mature, one of the primary areas where compatibility is important is in dealing with crisis. We all go through periods of growth, of trauma, of stress. But how we deal with these is vital to successful relationships. It is healthy and normal to be there for your friends when they go through trying times. But if they go through them much more often than you, if their "drama quotient" is higher than yours, then beware! You may end up being a caretaker, constantly riding their emotional bandwagon while having your own needs ignored.

For achieving healthy self-esteem, it's best to find friends and lovers who relate to the ups and downs of life in a way similar to yours—people with whom you ride the same roller coaster. Otherwise, you'll ultimately want to get off the ride and leave the park. And by then, you may be sick to your stomach.

Choosing people with common values and similar coping mechanisms will ensure a more satisfying journey together.

※ ※

Resolutions:

1. Clearly define your own needs and values in relationships. Outline your own strengths and weaknesses as well. There is no judgment here—just discovery.
2. Get to know your friends' and lover's needs and values, as well as their strong and weak points. You'll want to choose people whose outlook on life and daily coping skills are compatible with yours. This may take time—but it's worth it.
3. Remember that the way others present themselves to you very often does not show their true character. Get to know both their mask and their reality.

※ ※

COMMANDMENT IV

Trust thy body all the days of thy life (thy mind doth fornicate with thee).

Can you remember a time when you had just met someone and you had an immediate and overwhelming negative feeling about that person? Maybe your heart began to beat faster, or you felt nausea or anxiety, or you instinctively wanted to get away. At that point, did your mind jump in and try to save the day with thoughts like, "You shouldn't judge people so quickly," or, "Maybe they're just having a bad day"? And did you learn later that your initial gut reaction to that person was accurate?

Often, our considered reactions to other people are based on habits and patterns that we picked up from others, not our own instincts. Our parents taught us to be nice to relatives and friends we did not particularly like. Teachers blamed us for things that others did. Our religious counselors taught us that all people are good and we should never judge them. And yet how often have you discovered that the uncle who made you feel uneasy was actually a child molester, or that the new employee you just hired, whose résumé looked great but whose energy seemed "off" to you, is now causing problems in the office?

The result of all this programming from others is that our own "inner compass" is drowned out. We are all born with an innate intelligence, an inner knowing, that is our true source of guidance—especially when dealing with other people. This is a basic instinct that even animals share. In most cases, this intelligence speaks to us more accurately through our physical feelings and emotions than it does through our minds. Our minds have been so filled with false information and belief systems that it's hard for us to see and hear clearly.

Some years ago I was helping a friend of mine with a show he was producing. It was opening night, and my job was to usher in the guests and help them find their seats.

A man walked into the theater, and as soon as I saw him my body felt faint and my legs began to shake. I felt nauseated and weak, and as if I were about to pass out. Although I didn't understand the physical reaction my body was having, I knew that I had met this man somewhere before. I thought I had known him in some musical connection—perhaps we had done a show together.

After a few minutes of feeling faint and dizzy, I told my friend I had to sit down. As I was resting, this man walked by my seat and I asked him, "Don't I know you?" He looked at me, hedged a moment, then said, "No," and walked away.

Just then I remembered where I had known him. He was a professor at a community college where I had taught dance twenty years earlier. On Saturday afternoons, after my last class, I would often stop by his office to chat. We'd talk about shows, and sometimes he would play the guitar and we'd sing together. We would be the only two people in the building, and I would look forward to our philosophical discussions and our music.

One Saturday, he confided in me that he was lonely and longed for some company. As we were singing a song, he grabbed me, forced me to the floor, and tried to have sex with me. I fought him off and ran away.

Since then, I had pretty much forgotten about that incident. But when I saw him again, my body remembered it instantly.

Our bodies and feelings give us clues all the time, but often we are deaf to them because we are too busy with our thoughts, habits, and activities. Our minds have not been trained how to listen, how to be quiet enough to perceive our own inner guidance. Part of healthy self-esteem is learning to trust ourselves, to trust our instincts, to develop a rapport with our body and its messages. If we can learn to listen to our own inner self, then we will make healthier choices—and healthier choices are a major building block of self-esteem.

Resolutions:

1. Take a few minutes each day to do this simple but profound exercise. Sit comfortably in a chair, with your back straight, close your eyes, and begin to quiet your conscious mind. Bring all your thoughts to a point of stillness. It may help to focus on your breathing while doing this. Then once you've achieved that stillness, simply listen. Become aware of your body and how it feels. Learn to listen to its messages.

2. Then tune in to your feelings. Ask yourself what you are really feeling at the moment. Be honest with what is truly going on inside you—and develop a dialogue with that. Your feelings are a great way to access what's going on at your deepest level.

3. Then, as you go about your day, practice being aware of your body and feelings. As you meet people and situations, learn to be the observer of your self. Listen to your inner clues, be guided by them, and you will find your sense of personal power blossoming.

COMMANDMENT V

Thou hast permission at all times to say "NO," to change thy mind, and to express thy true feelings.

How often in your life have you been criticized for having the feelings you do? Did this make you feel invalidated? How often do you simply stuff your feelings and agree with others, saying "yes" when you really mean "no," just to keep the peace? And how does this make you feel afterward?

There is an old adage that "Good children make lousy adults." "Good" little boys and girls always follow the rules imposed on them by others. At some point in their development they need to declare their own sense of self, to express their own true thoughts and feelings. Adults with healthy self-esteem are able to express themselves freely, regardless of others' reactions. They are able to disagree, set their own boundaries, and maintain a strong sense of personal self.

Belle is a six-year-old girl who was participating in a pageant with some of her classmates. The show was a commemoration of spring, using poetry and music. The teacher, who is very artistic and a colleague of mine, chose the poem "Trees" as one of the selections.

In casting children for this piece, there were roles available for trees, two roles for rain, and one spot as a robin. To be fair in assigning the roles, the teacher decided to put each role on a piece of paper and have the children each draw one from a bowl. All the children agreed to this process.

Belle drew a role as a tree, but she wanted to be the robin. After she raised a fuss, it was explained to her that if she accepted the role, she would enjoy the rewards of a fun costume and singing and treats after the show. It was also explained that if she chose not to follow through with the agreement, then she could not be in the play or the festivities afterward.

With only a slight pause, Belle responded, "Okay, I won't be in the play." After that, she watched two rehearsals and sat through the final performance without one trace of a scowl, resentment, or regret. Peer pressure, treat pressure, and teacher pressure did not move her. She simply knew what she wanted, was able to say "no," and lived with her choice; from all outward indications she felt good about herself and the whole affair.

The reason we usually "give in" to others' feelings is that we have developed a fear of repercussions. Somewhere along our life's path, we got a message that our survival depended on our not expressing ourselves completely. And despite the fact that whatever negative circumstances existed then have likely changed by now, our brains are still operating under the old program. Consequently, it's much easier for us to just go along with others, to be a "yes" person, to blend in with our surroundings. And yet to do so is damaging to our self-esteem.

This brings us to the subject of risk. Healthy living involves healthy risking. So learning to speak up for ourselves becomes an important part of our well-being. This means facing our fear—of rejection, of disapproval, of not being accepted. And there is an ancient technique that can be of great value here—it's called "just doing it." Once we break through the fear, we begin to sense our personal power coming back. And just as we have built a habit of giving in, so we can create the habit of speaking out. Habits are built through repeated actions, coupled with strong desire. So, speak out! Be free to say, "Yes." Free to say, "No." Free to change your mind. Your self-esteem will love you for it.

Resolutions:

1. Become aware of the times in your life when you say "yes" but really mean "no."
2. Decide in each of these cases if you could suffer serious harm for disagreeing. If not, then muster up your courage and speak your truth. Observe your feelings afterward—and notice the direct link between speaking your mind and feeling personally empowered. Make the conscious choice to build this habit into your daily self-expression.
3. Practice changing your mind on a regular basis. Begin with minor events, such as making dinner or shaving, and proceed to more major issues. Although this may be considered "flaky behavior" in some circles, the ability to change one's mind is a very human trait and is an integral part of a healthy self-esteem.

COMMANDMENT VI

hat is not right for thee is also not right for thy brethren.

How many times have you heard someone say, "Our marriage was pretty unhappy; we fought a lot, but we stayed together for the sake of the kids"? Then when you talk with the "kids" (who are now most likely grown up) they may say they wished their parents had split up. In a well-meant effort to do what they thought was "right" for others they ended up doing something "wrong," injurious to both themselves and others. During the years of struggle the children could feel the discord more keenly than their parents knew. Whenever we make choices that are not appropriate for us "for the sake of others," those decisions may lead to conditions that are not appropriate for those others as well.

Being true to ourselves does not mean that we arrogantly follow whatever whim comes our way, at the expense of others. It does mean that we weigh very carefully how any decision involves our own well-being as well as that of others. When we first start practicing this commandment, it's common to feel "selfish." This is normal, and most people with low self-esteem need to feel what it's like to value themselves (remember that "ish" means "having a quality of, or touch of," so selfish merely means "having a sense of self"). And by learning to do what is right for us consistently, we begin to reclaim our self on a very deep level.

This may be the most difficult commandment to follow, because it involves choosing what's right for you—which implies having the faith that it will be right for others as well.

One of my clients, Laura, has four children—two girls and two boys. She began to notice how the children would try to pitch in and help her.

The oldest child, Meg, twelve, always volunteered to watch the baby. After some time of doing this, Meg came to her mother and said she had something to tell her. "Mom, I really like watching Jessica, but I'm tired of doing it so much. I feel like my brothers aren't doing their share. I feel bad about telling you this, but it's how I really feel. It doesn't feel fair to me."

Laura knew this was hard for Meg to say, because she was such a loving and caring daughter and sister. After talking the situation over with the whole family, it became apparent that it wasn't good for either Meg or her brothers for her to be watching the baby so often. The boys admitted that they felt left out of spending time with their younger sister.

So after this meeting the babysitting responsibilities were more equitably divided—and everyone felt better about it.

Being a martyr has no positive personal benefit. In fact, it's quite damaging to self-esteem. The world of a martyr is contracted, stagnant, and dark. The energy surrounding a person who is being true to himself or herself is expansive, centered, and bright. Shakespeare said it well: "To thine own self be true, and it must follow, as the night the day, thou canst not then be false to any man."

Resolutions:

1. Take inventory of your life. Discover areas in which you are being less than true to yourself.
2. Ask yourself the reasons why. Who do you think would be hurt if you were acting in your own best interest?
3. In those areas that involve others, make a written list of specific ways in which your life and theirs might be enhanced by your choosing what's best for you.

COMMANDMENT VII

Thou shalt not give beyond thine own capacity.

When was the last time you felt that your "well had run dry," that you had donated your very last drop of blood, sweat, and tears to someone else's need, that you had nothing left to give? You may have given of yourself mentally, emotionally, physically, or financially. In any case, you had overspent yourself and your resources and were now in a state of depletion.

If you analyzed just how you arrived at this state, you would notice that there was a point at which you crossed a line and began to give too much. You probably did not intend to do this, but were caught up in your own desire to help or were enmeshed in another's needs and entranced by the excitement of riding the wave. Perhaps you secretly hoped to be loved and appreciated for good and "selfless" effort.

Shannon, one of my clients, was struggling for several years. She lived from paycheck to paycheck, just barely getting by at the end of the month. She finally managed to save $250, which she set aside for emergencies. This gave her the first sense of security she'd known in years.

Soon afterward, one of her friends needed some money for an emergency—$250, to be exact. So Shannon lent her the money in her savings account. Two days later, Shannon's car needed a major part. She had to wait to get the money back from her friend before she could get her car out of the shop. And she lost income while waiting for the payback.

Shannon resolved never to lend out her last dollar again.

Healthy self-esteem allows us to give freely and frequently—but never to the point of our own depletion. Whether our gifts are mental, emotional, or physical, we share willingly, but always within our own established limits. These "boundaries" support us in preserving our energy and our healthy sense of self. Giving beyond these boundaries undermines our integrity, our self-esteem, and eventually our relationships.

There are many people in need, and many good causes to support. All of us have wounds in some areas that need healing—and if you have a good heart you will never lack for people around you wanting to be healed. The urge to serve and contribute is basic to human nature and should be honored—the trick is knowing when to stop. And this can be unclear because of parental, religious, and cultural conditioning.

An easy way to learn to stop is simply to view your mental, emotional, physical, and spiritual "selves" as bank accounts. Each day, you check your balances in these accounts before you "spend" one dime. Then you'll know just exactly how much you have to give and when you get too close to the line and need to stop giving.

Healthy self-esteem knows exactly where the line is—and prioritizes who receives the most (children or mate), who receives the rest, and how much is reserved for yourself, so that you may become a more effective, skillful giver.

Resolutions:

1. Examine your balance sheets (mental, emotional, physical, spiritual) on a daily or weekly basis.
2. Determine who is making the largest withdrawals in each account and whether this is appropriate. If necessary, write out your boundaries in each area and follow them.
3. As an exercise, choose a task where you are giving to a friend or social cause. Determine exactly where the line (of "too much") is—and then make the choice to stop at that very point. Notice how you feel inside—and how others react to you.

COMMANDMENT VIII

What thy brethren think of thee mattereth naught.

If you ask yourself the question, "How important to me are others' opinions of me?" your mind will probably respond, "Not much, really." But your emotions will probably have a very different answer. Perhaps you have a strong inner critic who reminds you constantly how you look and sound to others—it may even make you feel that they are constantly scrutinizing you and your behavior.

To be honest, we all have a certain investment in how others perceive us. Much of this we learned from an early age. Our parents looked at us critically as we tried to live up to their expectations. Our teachers viewed us critically as we tried to embody their lessons and ideals. Our friends were extremely critical as we tried hard to fit in with the "in crowd" and yet retain our individuality. And society, with its barrage of beautiful people in the media, gives us a definite standard by which to evaluate ourselves. Who can escape this gauntlet of opinions?

My sister, Kim, works at a senior adult community as a movement expression therapist. One day, some of the older residents were sitting around chatting with the attendants between scheduled activities. Kim was waiting to take them to an aquatic movement class.

One of the attendants gave an arthritic woman a stuffed animal to play with. Such activities tend to increase joint mobility. The woman cried: "Oh no, I don't want to hold this. Everyone is looking at me and they'll make fun of me because I'm playing with a child's toy."

A woman sitting next to her, who was known around the home for her spunk and vinegar, replied: "What the hell do you care who sees you with a toy? It's soft. It's cute. It's cuddly. Enjoy it until someone takes it away from you!"

When we learn to value ourselves, we are able to put others' opinions into truer perspective. We can then learn from others but not be so hurt by them. We can discriminate between people who are projecting their issues onto us and those who truly have our best interest at heart. We can listen to others' advice, decide what is true and helpful for us, and easily let go of the rest. We have the ability to find wisdom in others' lives and begin to embody it in our own. In short, we have healthy self-esteem.

It is important to distinguish between healthy and unhealthy criticism. The main difference here is one of motive. Most people will freely offer criticism that is essentially negative in content. A true friend will offer constructive advice, which is geared to our growth and betterment. Healthy self-esteem will choose carefully what it listens to, and easily ignores the naysayers and the critics. Eventually the strongest voice we listen to will be our own inner self and its deepest purpose.

Resolutions:

1. Sit down, close your eyes, and mentally review the opinions others have had of you. Make a list of all those that seem the most prominent in your mind.

2. Make note of which are constructive, which are not. Review the effect those opinions had, both positive and negative, on your behavior and on your success or failure.

3. Choose one area of your life in which you have certainty in your own belief. Mentally see yourself possessed of that belief. Feel it filling your body with its energy. Visualize yourself expressing that belief and acting on it in your life.

Take time to appreciate yourself for having that conviction, and love yourself as a strong individual. Then go out and express that belief to others and take some action on it. Notice how you feel.

COMMANDMENT IX

Wherever thou art, therein also is the party.

Can you recall a time when you were in school, your whole class was having a great day (going on a field trip, or decorating for the prom), and you were sick in bed at home with, say, strep throat? Do you remember lying in bed all day, thinking about all the fun you were missing? Do you still feel that the party is going on somewhere other than where you are?

Whenever you feel as if you're missing out on the action, as if you're not in the "right place," then you start to become "contracted." Over time, this can lead to depression, fatigue, and eroded self-esteem. You're almost never content, you're not able to be in the moment where you are. There is always a mythical somewhere else, some greener pasture where you're "supposed to be."

71

Many people run through life searching for that "right place," never knowing where it may be found. Occasionally, they may find a "right" job or a "right" partner—but before long some flaw will be found, and the search must continue. People who have this mind-set always seem to be searching, never finding; they are always en route, never arriving. Then one day they discover that, like the spider, their life is spun from inside themselves, from their own inner spirit. They are in the right place and now is the right time.

Healthy self-esteem believes that wherever you are is where the party is. "Party" does not mean just food, friends, and festivities—it means being in the right place. That can be with others, or it might mean being alone with yourself. People who believe that they are where the party is carry themselves with a certain strength and buoyancy through life. And they tend to magnetize wonderful, supportive events and people to themselves. They seem to have a resilience in dealing with uncomfortable situations.

One of my favorite stories is that of a friend's seven-year-old daughter. Whenever the family would go out for a drive in their car, she always wanted to sit in the front seat. And her father would have to tell her, "Whenever your mother is in the car, she gets to sit in the front seat and you must sit in the back." She never liked this and would always make a fuss. One day, she willingly jumped in the back seat without a word from Dad. He remarked to her, "Well, that's great—you didn't even have to be reminded to sit in the back." The daughter sat up straight and proudly asserted, "This is the front seat!"

Resolutions:

1. Write a time line of your life, noting the places you felt great about and the places you didn't feel great about (e.g., grade school, high school, home, camp, a particular job).
2. Check the percentage of places you felt were "right" for you vs. places you felt were leading to a "better place."
3. Realistically evaluate your ability to be in the moment and enjoy where you are. If you rate your ability for that as low, practice believing that wherever you are is the place to be and see how your self-esteem expands.

COMMANDMENT X

Thou shalt sing thine own praises all the days of thy life.

When you see a fantastic movie, do you tell your friends about it? When you discover a great restaurant, do you praise its cuisine to your coworkers? Most likely you do—it's natural to want to "share the good news." But how about when you do something wonderful? Do you give yourself credit for it? Probably not.

Most of us suffer from the habit of not valuing ourselves. We are very willing to praise others but unable to receive praise ourselves. We feel uncomfortable when others compliment us, as if we are being vain or self-centered. Many religions have taught that love of self is an unholy trait, a personal vice, whereas, in reality, true love of self is required for the practice of virtue. Healthy self-esteem is a prerequisite to being able to love and re-spect others.

All of us have an Inner Critic living inside of us. This is the voice that always looks at the bad, never the good; that instinctively sees what is lacking, not what is pre-sent; that recognizes only where we failed, not where we have triumphed. In many of us, this voice makes up most of our "self-talk," which governs largely how we feel about ourselves. And it's important to realize that this Inner Critic is a product of our past—we have uncon-sciously created it from the negative information we've been fed from our parents, friends, teachers, media, and the outside world. And because we've created it, we also have the power to dismantle it.

There is another voice inside us, one we might call the Protector. This is the voice of goodness. It supports our well-being, it nurtures us with thoughts of how tal-ented, kind, generous, loyal, or beautiful we really are. It acknowledges us when we do something right; and when we fall short, it brings us forgiveness and the resolve to improve.

Low self-esteem results when the Inner Critic prevails. So the key to high self-esteem is to practice focusing on the Protector. Whatever you put your attention on expands. So make friends with your Protector. Give it a shape, a size, a name—and give it continuous life within you, so that it may overrule your critic.

The Critic's job is to hurt the wounded child within you; the Protector's job is to nurture that wounded child's growth and development. Since both of these voices are literally "creatures of habit," you can choose your thoughts and feelings to be exactly what you wish. If you learn to focus on your best qualities at all times, realizing that under all circumstances you are doing your best given the obstacles you had to deal with, then you'll begin to see the face of the critic dissolving like the curtain before the Wizard of Oz. You will see clearly the lies and illusions you were fed and begin the most direct route to self-empowerment. Know that in reality you are the good, the true, and the beautiful—and that singing your praises is not only a healthy thing to do but is acknowledging who you really are!

During the time the movie *10* was popular, I was watching a TV special in which three actresses were being interviewed, one of whom was Bette Midler. And each actress was asked if she thought she rated a "10."

The first actress (who was an international sex symbol) replied, "I guess I'm at least an 8." The second (who was both an actress and a model) answered, "I suppose I'm a 7 or an 8." Bette Midler responded without a moment's hesitation: "10! Are you kidding? I'm a 57!"

※ ※

Resolutions:

1. As you go through each day, become very aware of the voices within you. Learn to recognize whenever your Critic is speaking, and when your Protector is talking to you. You may wish to keep a written journal of these "conversations."

2. Make it a daily practice to develop your Protector. Spend a few minutes each morning and evening learning to praise yourself and pay attention to your good qualities.

3. Seek out people, groups, workshops, or counselors who will assist you in embracing and developing your Protector. Surround yourself with people who make you feel good, who are willing to support your new commitment to becoming your best self.

※ ※

Self-Esteem Commitment

And so
I, one of the children of Earth,
Do commit to treat myself fairly,
Refusing to be a martyr or victim,
And will do my best to move forward in life
    with confidence and self-esteem.
Deep down I know this is my true design—
I am created in the image and likeness of
    the highest power that exists.
I embody this . . . I choose to love myself.
And so it is.
Amen.